I Ain't Never Been Nothing but a Winner

I Ain't Never Been Nothing but a Winner

Coach Paul "Bear" Bryant's
323 Greatest Quotes about Success, on and off the Football Field

Compiled by
CREED AND HEIDI TYLINE KING

TowleHouse Publishing Company
Nashville, Tennessee

This book is not an authorized work of the estate of Paul "Bear" Bryant. It is a compilation of Bryant quotes gathered by the authors from sources listed in this book's bibliography. The authors wish to thank University of Alabama and Bryant Museum officials for their assistance in the research of this book.

A contribution on behalf of Lee Roy Jordan has been paid by the publisher to the Bryant Museum.

TowleHouse books distributed by Cumberland House Publishing, 431 Harding Industrial Boulevard, Nashville, Tennessee 37211.

Library of Congress Cataloging-in-Publication Data

King, Heidi Tyline, 1966-
    I ain't never been nothing but a winner : coach Bear Bryant's 323 greatest quotes about success, on and off the football field / Heidi Tyline King and Creed King.
       p. cm.
    Includes bibliographical references and index.
    ISBN 0-9668774-2-X (hardcover : alk. paper)
    1. Bryant, Paul W.--Quotations. 2. Football--Quotations, maxims, etc. I. King, Creed, 1965- II. Title.

GV939.B+
796.332--dc21

                                                                00-026702

Page design by Mike Towle and Ed Curtis
Cover design by Gore Studio.

Printed in the United States of America

4 5 6—04 03 02 01

*In tribute to college football's greatest coach
and teacher, the Alabama family, and
William L. King Sr.—
our very own Bear Bryant*

FOREWORD

I had the great fortune to play football for Coach Bryant at the University of Alabama from 1959 through 1962. We won one national championship and barely missed winning another in those four seasons, during which time I learned lessons from Coach Bryant that continue to motivate and sustain me forty years later.

In reading this book, I took particular notice of one of his quotes about never quitting no matter how tough things are. That was particularly relevant for me back in the late 1980s. The economy wasn't good and business had taken a downturn. My lawyer was advising me to declare bankruptcy, but I knew that would be too much out of character for me, thinking back to the days when Coach Bryant had told me never to give up. A lot of people with more money than me were declaring bankruptcy, so I resolved to get up earlier, to stay late, and to outwork the competition. And that's exactly what I did to succeed.

Coach Bryant was quite a bright person, but he spoke in that deep, slow-talking drawl, so people were unaware of just how smart he really was. One thing about him was that his halftime locker-room speeches were never impromptu. During the week leading up to the game, he would prepare something to say if we were ahead and something else if we were behind. Sometimes he would be emotional; at other times he was very quiet and confident. He was a master at it. Coach Bryant would say something like, "These are the five things that we need to do,"— boom, boom, boom, boom, boom—and then we'd go out and make things happen.

He had a tremendous influence on me, just like he did with everyone. He always knew which guy needed a pat on the shoulder and which one needed a kick in the butt. Guys would be thinking about calling him names or how they didn't like football anymore, and twenty seconds later he'd have his hand on your shoulder, saying, "I really know you can be a leader, Lee Roy, and that you won't let me down," and that was all it took for me. His timing was impeccable, every time.

I think back now on how fantastic it was to have had all those opportunities to be with him. There's so much good stuff in this book for people to glean from and apply to their own lives and relationships. It's down-to-earth, common-sense things that he believed would inspire play-ers to great accomplishments. Don't just read this book— listen to Coach Bryant, and savor what he says. I sure do.

—*Lee Roy Jordan*

INTRODUCTION

PAUL "BEAR" BRYANT, THE winningest coach in major college football history, was more than a mastermind at the game. He was a motivator. He believed that hard work, dedication, and self-confidence were the traits that rescued him from a life of "plowing and driving those mules and chopping cotton for fifty cents a day." They were the keys to success both on and off the playing field, and he considered it his job to instill such characteristics in his players. "Lessons can be taught in football that are difficult to get across in the home, church, or classroom," he said. "It's my pleasure as a coach to watch a young man apply these lessons later in life."

Bryant was born September 11, 1913, in Moro Bottom, Arkansas, the eleventh of twelve children. His father was a semi-invalid, and as his older brothers left home, Bryant had to shoulder much of the responsibility and chores that came with farming 260 acres. He plowed barefoot, milked cows, chopped cotton, and peddled produce with his mother in nearby Fordyce. His childhood was hard, but it was also a happy one filled with boyish pranks like the shenanigan that earned him his nickname, "Bear." On a bet, the twelve-year-old wrestled a bear. Although Bryant pinned the bear, he never collected his money. The nickname stuck, however, and Bryant basked in the attention.

Another defining characteristic of his childhood was the devotion and love between mother and son. As a coach, he emphasized to players the importance of keeping in touch, and he thought it was healthy for every one of them to "find time to write their mother and go see their mother." Years later, while saying his lines in the now-famous television commercial he made for a telephone company, Bryant asked, "Have you called your mama lately?" Then he replied impromptu, "I sure wish I could call mine."

While Bryant was ashamed of being poor and embarrassed by the stigmas that it imposed upon him, his childhood ultimately shaped him into the man he would become. His size made him a natural for football, and he used the sport as a means to escape poverty and life as a farmer. His father didn't want him to play football, but his mother turned her head the other way, and in high school he developed into an all-state player. His team, the Fordyce Redbugs, won back-to-back state football championships—in 1929 and 1930. Bryant's performance attracted scouts from several colleges. Ultimately, he chose Alabama for the attention—everybody in the South had heard of the Crimson Tide.

Bryant earned three varsity letters playing for the Tide, and he was part of two conference championship teams and the 1934 national championship team. His most memorable game came during his senior season, when he played with a broken leg against Tennessee. The game was among his best, and Bama beat the Volunteers, 25-0. It was also as an undergraduate that he met and married Mary Harmon Black, "the best-looking gal you or I have ever laid eyes on."

B RYANT BEGAN his coaching career with a short stint at Union College in Jackson, Tennessee, followed by three years as an assistant coach at Alabama and two years as an assistant at Vanderbilt. After World War II broke out, he enlisted in the service and spent the next four years in the navy, serving time in North Africa and the North Carolina Pre-Flight Training at Chapel Hill, where he coached football until the war ended.

After the war he landed his first job as a head coach. That was at the University of Maryland, where he turned around a program that had won only one game the year before to a 6-2-1 team. But he didn't stay there long. After the school president fired a coach in Bryant's absence and reinstated a

player that had been kicked off the team, Bryant left
Maryland, promising himself he would never allow
similar circumstances to occur.

Bryant went to the University of Kentucky in
1946 and coached the Wildcats for eight seasons.
During Bryant's tenure, the Wildcats posted eight
consecutive winning seasons, won four bowl games,
and captured the school's first conference
championship in football. He remains, even today,
the school's winningest football coach, with sixty
victories. Bryant probably could have finished his
coaching career in Lexington, but that would have
meant having to play second fiddle in a state
where basketball reigned No. 1. He also didn't like
being in the shadow of Adolph Rupp, and after a
fiercely contested battle, he was allowed to break
his contract.

Bryant's next stop was College Station, Texas,
home of the Texas A&M Aggies. A&M wasn't his
first choice for a new assignment, but it was the only
one with a head-coach opening suitable for him.
During his inaugural (1954) season in College
Station, Bryant took the team to Junction City for

what proved to be a brutal training camp. His practices were so rigorous that Bryant returned trailed by a bedraggled bunch of misfits who somehow managed to tough it out—including future Crimson Tide coach Gene Stallings. Bryant's first A&M team struggled to a 1-9 season, but he managed to build winning teams the following three years, including a Southwest Conference champion in 1956. A year later John David Crow became Bryant's only Heisman Trophy winner.

In 1958, Bryant was named head coach at Alabama. Commenting on his return to his alma mater, Bryant said it was "like when you were out in the field and you heard your mama calling you to dinner. Mama called." It was the beginning of a twenty-five-year reign at Bama—one that made him a legend in college football. It also turned him into Alabama's favorite son—so much so that even today, people are still naming their children after Paul "Bear" Bryant.

B RYANT'S CAREER coaching accomplishments were phenomenal. They included 323 victories (more than any other coach in Division I college football history), twenty-nine bowl appearances—including twenty-four straight—in thirty-eight seasons, national coach-of-the-year honors in 1961, 1971, and 1973, two coach-of-the-decade honors, six national championships (Associated Press titles in 1961, 1964, 1965, 1978, 1979, and a separate United Press International championship in 1973), and twenty-five conference titles.

Bryant retired in 1982 after a victory in the Liberty Bowl against Illinois. Shortly thereafter, on January 26, 1983, he passed away. Flags across the state flew at half-staff, and a line of fans stretched almost the entire distance from Tuscaloosa to Birmingham, where he was buried.

While football made a name for Bryant, his legacy to the players, coaches, and fans who knew and followed him is the way he turned football into an analogy for life. Today, almost twenty years after his death, people across the country continue to use Bryant's words of wisdom as encouragement in their lives. He often said that "Mama wanted me to be a preacher. I told her coachin' and preachin' were a lot alike."

How right he was.

I Ain't Never
Been Nothing but
a Winner

This is the beginning of a new day.
God has given me this day to use as I will.
I can waste it or use it for good.
What I do today is very important because I am
  exchanging a day of my life for it.
When tomorrow comes, this day will be gone
  forever,
Leaving something in its place I have traded for it.
I want it to be a gain, not loss—good, not evil.
Success, not failure, in order that
I shall not forget the price I paid for it.

—W. W. Heartsill Wilson

(Tram Sessions, a former legislator from Birmingham, sent this quote to Bryant. It became one of his favorites, and he kept a tattered copy in his wallet.)

ABILITY

1. Players can be divided, roughly, into four types. Those who have ability and know it, those who have it and don't know it, those who don't have it and know it, and those who don't have it but don't know it.

2. The ones who have ability and don't use it are the ones who eat your guts out. I've messed up my share of those.

3. There's no use fussing on a boy who doesn't have any ability.

4. Don't ever give up on ability. Don't give up on a player who has it.

5. Those in-betweeners, I'm a champion with them.

6. A good, quick, small team can beat a big, slow team any time.

ADMIRATION

7. They make me look ridiculous but the fans get a kick out of it, so what does it matter? The jokes are silly, but they don't offend me—anything to sell tickets.

(Bryant referring to admiring fans)

Bear Bryant in 1948, his third year as coach of the Kentucky Wildcats. (AP/Wide World Photos)

ADVERSITY

8. I have always tried to teach my players to be fighters. When I say that, I don't mean put up your dukes and get in a fistfight over something. I'm talking about facing adversity in your life. There is not a person alive who isn't going to have some awfully bad days in their lives. I tell my players that what I mean by fighting is when your house burns down, and your wife runs off with the drummer, and you've lost your job and all the odds are against you. What are you going to do? Most people just lay down and quit. Well, I want my people to fight back.

9. You never know how a horse will pull until you hook him to a heavy load.

10. Keep your head up; act like a champion.

11. In life, you'll have your back up against the wall many times. You might as well get used to it.

12. Coming from behind is still one of the greatest lessons, and the ability to do it is the mark of a great team.

13. If you get knocked down, get up.

AGE

14. You're never too old until you think you are.

15. Age has nothing to do with it. You can be out of touch at any age.

ALABAMA

16. I know this much: Alabama football will survive anything, because we play the most interesting football there is—we win.

17. I had no doubt we would win at Alabama. I just didn't know how long it would take.

18.
In Alabama, football is a way of life.

19. And I always say this: Because of our program they'll wind up better people in the three important areas of life—mental, physical, and spiritual.

20. It was like when you were out in the field and you heard your mama calling you to dinner. Mama called.

(On why he came to Alabama)

21. I just want to thank God for giving me the opportunity to coach at my alma mater and be part of the University of Alabama tradition.

22. I don't doubt for a minute that those '64, '65, and '66 Alabama teams will be remembered as much for their size as for their achievements. The first two won the national championships, and the third should have won it because it was undefeated and untied and the best team in the country that year. I don't care what the Notre Dame people say, we were the best.

23. If you want an education and you want to be a great football player, this is the place for you. I know we can coach you. If you're not interested in those two things, then we have nothing in common.

24. The only president who's ever been fired at Alabama was against football. Any new president cuts his teeth on it, and he better be for it. Because if he's not, they won't win, and if they don't win, he'll get fired.

25. In Alabama, you better be for football or you might as well leave.

ATTITUDE

26. Smile. You'll catch a lot more bugs if you smile than you will with vinegar.

27. It's a lot better to be seen than heard. The sun is the most powerful thing I know of, and it doesn't make much noise.

28. I think the most important thing of all for any team is a winning attitude. The coaches must have it. The players must have it. The student body must have it. If you have dedicated players who believe in themselves, you don't need a lot of talent.

29. If a man has the right attitude, even if he is average, he'll work hard enough to play well. As long as he thinks he can be good, that's all that counts.

30. If they don't have a winning attitude, I don't want them.

31. The point is that you just can't cry when it's no good crying.

32. You don't change people's thinking overnight.

33. Winning isn't imperative, but coming from behind and getting tougher in the fourth quarter is. I don't want you to think you have to win, because you don't. On the other hand, if you can go out there ripping and snorting and having fun by knocking people around, I assure you—you will win!

34. Every man I had left on the team felt he could whip Joe Louis on Saturday. The difference between winning and losing is attitude.

(On his Junction Boys at Texas A&M)

35. After the game there are three types of people. One comes in and he ain't played worth killing and he's lost. And he gets dressed and out of there as quick as he can. He meets his girl and his mama, and they ain't too damn glad to see him. And he goes off somewhere and says how "the coach shoulda done this or that," and "the coach don't like me," and "I didn't play enough." And everybody just nods.

    And the second type will sit there a while, thinking what he could have done to make his team a winner. And he'll shed some tears. He'll finally get dressed, but he doesn't want to see anybody. His mama's out there. She puts on a big act and tells him what a great game he played, and he tells her if he had done this or that he'd be a winner, and that he will be a winner—next week.

And then there's the third guy. The winner. He'll be in there hugging everybody in the dressing room. It'll take him an hour to dress. And when he goes out it's a little something extra in it when his daddy squeezes his hand. His mama hugs and kisses him, and that little old ugly girl snuggles up, proud to be next to him. And he knows they're proud. And why.

36.
Be yourself.
Don't try to copy anyone else.

AUBURN

37. At Alabama one morning at seven, I placed a call from my office to Shug Jordan or somebody at Auburn, and the girl said nobody was in yet. I said, "What's the matter, honey, don't you people take football seriously?"

38. I know one thing: I'd rather die now than to have died this morning and missed this game.

(After Alabama's 31-7 win over unbeaten Auburn in 1971)

39.
Sure I'd love to beat Notre Dame, don't get me wrong. But nothing matters more than beating that cow college on the other side of the state!

40. I'm happy for them. Pat and Auburn had a fine year. I wanted him to get off to a good start, but not too good of a start. He'd get all biggity.

     (Congratulating Pat Dye on a good season in 1981)

41. To be honest, they soon copy everything we do. As an example, they were using those big, burly boys and we beat 'em with little quick ones. They switched to the little quick ones and we went to the big ones and beat 'em some more. Now they're back to the big ones. It's flattering, actually.

42. Our winning drive was one of the finest I've ever seen. We had to have it. I'm just thrilled to death with the win. We've got some mighty fine plowhands on this team.

     (Bryant's comment after the 1979 game. Auburn students were yelling, "Plow, Bear, plow," before the game—their response to his comment about having to go back to Arkansas and plow if Bama lost to Auburn)

AVOIDING MISTAKES

43. Don't get penalties. Don't break assignments. Most penalties are carelessness. Coach so they don't get penalties. One Alabama team went ten games without a fifteen-yard penalty. Don't fumble. A fumble is worse than an interception. Let the ball carrier carry the ball in the strong arm.

BALANCE

44. You don't strive for sameness, you strive for balance.

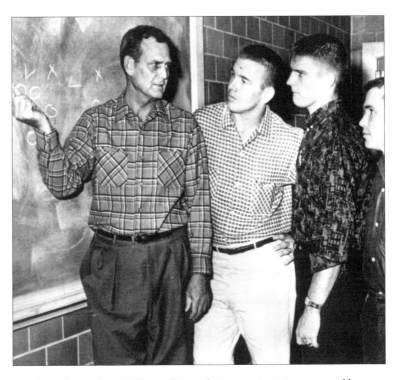

It is December 1959, and Coach Bryant is giving some of his Crimson Tide players a chalk talk heading into that year's Liberty Bowl game against Penn State. (AP/Wide World Photos)

CHARACTER

45. The one that makes you proud is the one who isn't good enough to play, but it means so much to him, he puts so much into it, that he plays anyway. I have had a lot of those, and I can coach them better than most.

46. The biggest mistake coaches make is taking borderline cases and trying to save them. I'm not talking about grades now, I'm talking about character. I want to know before a boy enrolls about his home life, and what his parents want him to be. And I want him to know the criterion at Alabama is up on my office wall in those four-color pictures.

    (Referring to championship photographs)

47. You just can't tell about left-handed crapshooters and quarterbacks . . .

    (Referring to Kenny Stabler)

48. I have tried to teach them to show class, to have pride, and to display character. I think football, winning games, takes care of itself if you do that.

CLASS

49. I don't know what class is, but I can tell when one has it. You can tell it from a mile away.

50. I always want my players to show class, knock 'em down, pat them on the back, and run back to the huddle.

51. Keep your poise.

COACHING

52. Mama wanted me to be a preacher. I told her coachin' and preachin' were a lot alike.

53. The first thing a football coach needs when he is starting out is a wife who is willing to put up with a whole lot of neglect. The second thing is at least a five-year contract.

54. Show me a football coach who shoots good golf and I'll show you a horse-sh— coach.

55. Coaches are teachers, and they teach many an important lesson to these young men. I've seen many a boy grow into a man by playing football.

56. The best coaches, most coaches I've known, weren't Phi Beta Kappa in the classroom.

57. But it's still a coach's game. Make no mistake. You start at the top. If you don't have a good one at the top, you don't have a cut dog's chance. If you do, the rest falls into place. You have to have good assistants, and a lot of things, but first you have to have the chairman of the board.

58. Another rule I believe in: I don't have any ideas, my coaches have them. I just pass the ideas on and referee the arguments.

59. Stay organized and keep things simple.

60. Learn to recognize winners.

61. I tell young players who want to be coaches, who think they can put up with all the headaches and heartaches, "Can you live without it? If you can't live without it, don't get in it."

62. A coach is stupid if he doesn't do what is best for his people.

63. I don't pay any attention to a coach. I've never seen a coach win a game yet.

64. A good high school coach does more real coaching and recruiting than anybody.

65. The old lessons (work, self-discipline, sacrifice, teamwork, fighting to achieve) aren't being taught by many people other than football coaches these days. The football coach has a captive audience and can teach these lessons because the communication lines between himself and his players are more wide open than between kids and parents. We better teach these lessons or else the country's future population will be made up of a majority of crooks, drug addicts, or people on relief.

COMEBACKS

66. It proves to our players that they have class and character.

67. Winning isn't imperative, but getting tougher in the fourth quarter is.

68. They displayed a lot of character and class. In doing that, when they get out in life making a living or doing whatever they're doing, if they get into a tough spot, they know they can do that.

(Comments after winning game No. 315 to surpass Amos Alonzo Stagg's record for career victories)

COMMITMENT

69. I don't want ideas just thrown out, I want them thought out.

70. They played like it was a sin to give up a point.
    (Referring to Alabama's defense in 1962, which yielded only twenty-two points during the regular season)

COMPROMISE

71. Never compromise with what you think is right.

CONFIDENCE

72. As long as you know within yourself—and the guys with you know it—that you have confidence in the plan, you know you are not going to fail.

73. If he'd kicked it straight, we would have blocked it.
    (After Tennessee's missed field goal in 1966 game; the Tide won in Knoxville 11-10)

74. They think they're good enough to win, and they go out and win.

75. There flies a dead duck.
    (Bryant's comment to former USC coach John McKay after shooting and missing a duck while hunting)

COURAGE

76. There's no substitute for guts.

77. What we gotta do is suck our own guts up—not depend on someone else to lose theirs.

78. Have courage.

79. Don't give up. Reach down inside of you and you'll find something left.

80. It's an old story. You stick your head above the crowd, and you're going to have people trying to knock it off.

COURTESY

81. Mama told me to never wear a hat indoors.
    (Bryant's answer when asked why he didn't wear his houndstooth hat
    for the 1976 Sugar Bowl)

82. I don't make a lot of rules for my players. I
    expect them to act like gentlemen, to have
    good table manners, to be punctual, to be
    prayerful. I expect them to be up on their
    studies, and I don't expect them to be
    mooning around the campus holding hands
    with the girls all the time, because that
    comes later, when they're winners. In a war,
    what do the losers get?

CRISIS

83. In a crisis, don't hide behind anything or anybody. They're going to find you anyway.

CRITICS

84. As far as the critics, well, they don't know what the hell they're talking about. Most of them have ridden their daddies' coattails and haven't done a thing on their own anyway.

85. The alumni are starting to grumble, and I'm the one starting it. *(After a close loss)*

DECISIONS

86. If you start to make a decision, go ahead and make it. Don't mealy-mouth around.

DESIRE

87. You're still going to win with preparation and dedication and plain old desire. If you don't have genuine desire, you won't be dedicated enough to prepare properly.

DETERMINATION

88. Don't give up before the game starts. I lost a Kentucky game with Georgia in 1946 simply because I didn't believe we could win.

89. Put everything you've got into anything you do.

90. There are three types of football players. First, there are those who are winners and know they are winners. Then there are the losers who know they are losers. Then there are those who are not winners but don't know it. They're the ones for me. They never quit trying. They're the soul of our game.

91. Don't give up on yourself. How you do this fall [season] will go a long way in shaping your life, and don't you ever doubt it.

(Speech given to incoming players)

DISCIPLINE

92. When you're teaching a boy to work for the first time in his life and teaching him to sacrifice and suck up his guts when he's behind, which are lessons he has to learn sooner or later, you are going to find boys who are not willing to pay the price.

93. Do things you don't like to do; bear down that much harder on what you hate doing. It'll make you a lot better player. And a lot better person.

94. If you don't learn anything but self-discipline, then athletics is worthwhile.

95. Don't ruin a practice by not disciplining yourself. If you're upset, don't take it out on your team.

96. If you don't have discipline, you can't have a successful program.

97. Be good or be gone.

(Sign in Bryant's office at Kentucky)

EXCUSES

98. The same things win today that have always won, and they will win years from now. The only difference is the losers have a whole new bunch of excuses why they don't win or can't win.

A downcast Bryant tries to console star quarterback Joe Namath after the Crimson Tide's loss to Texas in the 1965 Orange Bowl. (AP/Wide World Photos)

EXPECTATIONS

99. We betray our people if we fail to demand a winning attitude and the full cooperation of all concerned in all areas.

FAIRNESS

100. When I was a young coach I used to say, "Treat everybody alike." That's bull. Treat everybody fairly.

101. Everybody is different. If you treat them all alike you won't reach them. Be fair with all of them and you have a chance. One you pat on the back, and he'll jump out the window for you. Another you kick in the tail. A third you yell at and squeeze a little. But be fair. And that's what I am.

102. You can't treat them all equally, but you can treat them fairly.

FAITH

103. Never be too proud to get down on your knees and pray.

FAMILY LIFE

104. Every time a player goes out there, at least twenty people have some amount of influence on him. His mother has more influence than anyone. I know because I played, and I loved my mama.

105. There ought to be a special place in heaven for coaches' wives.

106. If the mother's for you, not much can be against you.

     (Speaking about a recruit's mother)

107. When we have a good team, I know it's because we have boys that come from good mamas and papas.

108. Have you called your mama lately? Sure wish I could call mine.

     (Television commercial for a telephone service)

109. I have let football rob me of some valuable time that I should have been spending with her [my wife] and with my daughter and my son.

110. Write home. Everyone should find time to write their mother and go see their mother. I think that's healthy.

FINANCIAL SUCCESS

111. It takes a lot of pressure off if you're not broke.

112. Sure, being hungry could be a great motivator, but coaching is a lot more fun if you don't have to do it for a living.

113. Nobody makes any money coaching football. You do well if you can break even and live in a style that's comfortable for you.

FOOTBALL

114. There are a lot of lessons in football that are very difficult to teach in the home, in the church, or in the classroom. They're easy to teach on the football field, and if the players don't learn these lessons, then football is not very worthwhile. The lessons are simple: first of all there's work and sacrifice; you have to do a lot of that. Then there's discipline. Then comes teamwork and cooperation. I've read a lot about successful men. They don't do it alone. It always takes a team.

115. If you're caught with a weak team, don't try to get fancy and please the spectators. The weaker you are, the more conservatively you must play. You play that way and you might win. At least you'll be respectable.

116. Only three things can happen on a pass play and two of them are bad.

117.
Offense sells tickets. Defense wins games.

118. I want to have my best offensive and defensive units rested and fresh just before the half. I want them not to be worn down for the first five minutes of the second half, and I want them fresh for the last ten minutes of the game. These are the times that football games are won and lost.

119. The first year doesn't count when you're on a five-year plan because you're playing with someone else's material.

120. I believe that football can teach you to sacrifice, to discipline yourself.

121. What else have we got to anchor to? Where else can we walk out there even, same everything, even, and compete? Look around. Maybe the football field's the only place left. Maybe we've already lost it everywhere else.

122. Football is different things to different people. For everybody I know it's something to tie to. Everybody can't tie to an English class. Everybody can tie to a football team.

123. Some coaches have accused me of being too defense-minded, but most of those who said that have wound up being athletic directors.

124. What are you doing here? Tell me why you are here. If you are not here to win a national championship, you're in the wrong place. You boys are special. I don't want my players to be like other students. I want special people. You can learn a lot on the football field that isn't taught in the home, the church, or the classroom. There are going to be days when you think you've got no more to give and then you're going to give plenty more. You are going to have pride and class. You are going to be very special. You are going to win the national championship for Alabama.

(Bryant's first meeting with his first team at Alabama in 1958)

125. I have never felt for a minute that football is the reason an institution exists, or that it is the most important reason. But I don't doubt its importance as a rallying point. It's pretty tough to rally around a math class.

126. It would be better if they opened it up. Give every team a chance to go to any bowl.

    (On bowl selections)

127. TV exposure is so important to our program and so important to this university that we will schedule ourselves to fit the medium. I'll play at midnight, if that's what TV wants.

FRIENDS

128. There's another tip-off for you, the kind of people you tie to.

GAME DAY

129. I don't care how much talent a team has— if the boys don't think tough, practice tough, and live tough, how can they play tough on Saturday?

130. If you're ahead, play like you're behind and if you're behind, play like you're ahead.

131. Don't do a lot of coaching just before the game. If you haven't coached them by fourteen minutes to two on Saturday, it's too late then.

132. My favorite play is the one where the player pitches the ball back to the official after scoring a touchdown.

GAME PLAN

133. I'm no innovator. If anything I'm a stealer, or borrower. I've stolen or borrowed from more people than you can shake a stick at.

134. Don't change your game plan unless you have to. Certainly, you've got to have a plan that's flexible. Don't change when it isn't necessary.

GOALS

135. Have a plan in your life and be able to adjust it. Have a plan when you wake up, what you're going to do with your day. Just don't go lollygagging through any day of your life. I hope I have had some luck in my life because I have planned for the good times and the bad ones.

136. First year, a .500 season. Second year, a conference championship. Third year, undefeated. Fourth, a national championship. And by the fifth year, we'll be on probation, of course.

137. I'm not saying we'll win any games, but I will say that the only thing that will satisfy us is to win twelve.

138. Have a goal. And to reach that goal, you'd better have a plan. Have a plan that you believe in so strongly you'll never compromise.

139. Set a goal, adopt a plan that will help you to achieve the goal. Chances of things happening in this world without goals are slim. Make sure that the goal means a lot to you. Believe that the plan is going to win. Tie to people who believe in the plan.

140. Make sure that your plan makes the player a better person. If it doesn't, you're just using people and the plan can't be worth much.

141. Set goals—high goals for you and your organization. When your organization has a goal to shoot for, you create teamwork, people working for a common good.

Coach Bryant goes the Western-wear route to the apparent delight of
Texas A&M coach and Bryant protégé Gene Stallings prior to the
1968 Cotton Bowl game. (AP/Wide World Photos)

GOLF

142. I was invited to Augusta to play the Masters course. I played twenty-seven holes and that little par-three [course]. I told Joe Namath how thrilled I was to play there. He said me playing over there was like taking a pig to the beauty parlor.

HABITS

143. I still get up at five o'clock. I'd like to sleep later but after thirty-seven years in this business I find I can't. To me it's still time wasted when you sleep past six.

HAPPINESS

144. Little things make me proud.

145. There is no sin in not liking to play; it's a mistake for a boy to be there if he doesn't want to.

HARD WORK

146. I'm not as smart as other coaches; I have to work harder.

(When asked why he had to get up at five o'clock)

147. I'm no miracle man. I guarantee nothing but hard work.

148.

Work hard. There is no substitute for hard work. None. If you work hard, the folks around you are going to work harder. If you drag into work late, what kind of impression is that going to leave on your fellow workers? If you leave early, what kind of impression is that going to leave?

149. Listen, does your boy know how to work? Try to teach him to work, to sacrifice, to fight. He better learn now, because he's going to have to do it someday.

150. Football has been a road out of poverty for many a young man. When you don't have anything to go back to, then, by gosh, you're going to work a little harder.

151. You learn to work. You have to work hard to succeed in anything.

152. Don't overwork your squad. If you're going to make a mistake, under-work them.

153. Be aware of "yes" men. Generally, they are losers. Surround yourself with winners. Never forget—people win.

154. Get people who work for your organization because it means something to them. Most organizations get people who are interested in drawing their paycheck for their forty-hour week. Don't forget, those folks usually don't work but about ten hours out of the forty they are paid for. To be the best—if you want to be the best—get people who care about your institution, people who are proud to be associated with your organization. Get winning people.

HEART

155. Bigness is in the heart.

HIMSELF

156. Woody is a great coach, and I ain't bad.

(After victory over Woody Hayes's Ohio State team, 35-6, in 1978 Sugar Bowl)

157. As long as I'm right, I don't give a damn what people think.

158. You can learn a lot on the football field that isn't taught in the home, in the church, or in the classroom. I'm a pretty good example of that.

159. Football has never been just a game to me. Never. I knew it from the time it got me out of Moro Bottom, Arkansas—and that's one of the things that motivated me, that fear of going back to plowing and driving those mules and chopping cotton for fifty cents a day.

160. I don't know why you people keep making such a big deal over Woody Hayes and Paul Bryant. I can assure you I'm not going to play and I hope Woody does.

(On the 1978 Sugar Bowl matchup)

161. All my life I'd wanted to coach at Southern Cal. Why, in Los Angeles, I'd been bigger than John Wayne! Wouldn't you know, Southern Cal offered me a job on the Sunday after I'd signed a contract with Texas A&M on Saturday.

162. I don't want to be the greatest coach in the world. I just want to walk off the field a winner.

163. All I know is I don't want to stop coaching and I don't want to stop winning, so we're gonna break the record unless I die. As long as somebody has to be the winningest coach, heck, it might as well be me.

164. I'm no genius. But I'm a damn good football coach.

165. I'm sick and tired of hearing Paul Bryant, Paul Bryant. I'm tired of hearing 315. I've lost a lot more games than I've won. Players win games.

166. Is work fun? I love to go to practice, I get a thrill every time I walk on that field. I thank the good Lord every day I walk on that field. I get a big letdown after the game is over. After the bowl game, it takes two to three days for it to sink in that the season is over.

167. I'm through tiptoeing around, and I'm through pussyfooting around. I'm going back to being Paul Bryant, and anybody who doesn't like the way Paul Bryant does things can get the heck out of here.

HUMILITY

168. Be humble. It's awfully easy for an athlete to get so wrapped up in himself that he doesn't know what's going on around him. I get more publicity than anybody around the university, but there are a lot of people there more important than I am. I think about that every day.

INFLUENCE

169. Take any winning team, any winning player, check him out and find out how many people had an influence on him being a player—his parents, his high school coaches, his teachers, his friends—and multiply that by sixteen.

170.

I don't try to save the world. I just go at it one football player at a time.

INITIATIVE

171. Make something happen.

KEEPING YOUR COOL

172. Don't talk too much. Don't pop off. Don't talk after the game until you cool off.

173. Don't talk too much or too soon.

LAZINESS

174. Don't tolerate lazy people. They are losers. People who come to work and watch clocks and pass off responsibilities will only drag you and your organization down. I despise clock watchers. They don't want to be part of a winning situation. They won't roll up their sleeves when you need them to. If you have lazy people, get rid of them. Remember, it is easy to develop the bad habits of lazy people.

LEADERSHIP

175. Find your own picture, your own self in anything that goes bad. It's awfully easy to mouth off at your staff or chew out players, but if it's bad, and you're the head coach, you're responsible. If we have an intercepted pass, I threw it. I'm the head coach. If we get a punt blocked, I caused it. A bad practice, a bad game, it's up to the head coach to assume his responsibility.

176. Over the years I've learned a lot about coaching staffs, and the one piece of advice I would pass on to a young head coach—or a corporation executive or even a bank president—is this: Don't make them in your image. Don't even try. My assistants don't look alike, think alike, or have the same personalities. And I sure don't want them all thinking like I do.

177. You don't have to talk a lot to be a leader. Lee Roy Jordan was a great leader, and he never said a word. But if he grunted, everybody listened.

178. Football changes and so do people. The successful coach is the one who sets the trend, not the one who follows it.

179. The idea of molding men means a lot to me.

180. You can't throw a fit once a month, go down and shake somebody, and impress him very much. They think, who the hell is this? You're like a shower coming down. Just wait and it goes away. If you're in the trenches with them every day, they'll do anything you want.

181. I can reach a kid who doesn't have any
     ability as long as he doesn't know it.

182. All I do is kind of run the ship. Me, I'm just
     a rural old boy who's been around a long
     time and is not all that bright, to be honest
     about it. But we'll try to give them a
     football game.

183. Leaders are self-starters. They say, "Let's go"
     and lead. They don't say, "Sic 'em" and step
     back to watch the fighters do the work.

LEARNING

184. Learn from others. Ask questions. Be a
     good listener. Get a pulse beat of what is
     going on around you.

LEVEL PLAYING FIELD

185. Sport is the only place we have left where we can start even.

186. We're supposed to be living in a very sophisticated time; with sophisticated young people. All worldly wise and knowledgeable. How can the game of football still be important in that context? I'll tell you how I feel. I feel it's more important than ever.

LIFE

187. You can learn from anybody.

188. I think anyone is wrong to get involved in one thing so completely all his life like I have. You get to a point when thirty minutes after the last game you start thinking about the next one. That's not all there is in life.

Bear Bryant in 1971, apparently contemplating another run at a national title. (AP/Wide World Photos)

LOSING

189. When you win, there's glory enough for everybody. When you lose, there's glory for none.

190. It's awfully important to win with humility. It's also important to lose. I hate to lose worse than anyone, but if you never lose you won't know how to act. If you lose with humility, then you can come back.

191. Like I said, though, I don't really consider it a loss. We just ran out of time.
    (On losing to Notre Dame in the 1973 Sugar Bowl, 24-23)

192. What happens today you'll have to live with the rest of the way. You can't get it back if you don't win. It's sixty minutes and over. The losers are the ones who say, "Oh, I wish I could play it again." You can't play it again.

193. I'm not interested in moral victories. That's too much like kissing your sister. I'm interested in winning, and all this stuff about building character with a losing team is a bunch of tommyrot.

194. Maybe the good Lord is kinda testing us to see what we got in us.

195. I'm not trying to tell you I told you so—but I'll tell you like I always try to tell you and like any coach will tell you, ten minutes after the game, it's too late. The next day is too late. So the best thing we can do is to use this as a stepping-stone, and if we've got class, we'll be all right. If we haven't, then it doesn't matter, does it?

196. Losing doesn't make me want to quit. It makes me want to fight that much harder.

197. In a way, it was a nightmare. The team had very little ability, but my, what character! They could have given up a hundred times—but they didn't. And I firmly believe that—if I had done a better job—we wouldn't have lost at Texas A&M. We were losing games by three and four and six points. What do you do? That's what is still eating my heart out. I just don't know the answer.

LOYALTY

198. Always be totally loyal to the institution for which you work. If you don't have the best interest of the organization at heart or if you can't be loyal, you are in the wrong place.

199. Always be totally loyal to your staff. If you are, then they'll be loyal back. Remember loyalty and honesty are two-way streets. If you are ever dishonest to members of your staff, you'll never regain their respect.

LUCK

200. Nothing happens by accident. You make your own luck.

MENTORING

201. I remember so well, after I played my last
     game, how alone I felt, and I want my boys
     to always feel they can come to me. And I'll
     say this, you can learn as much from them as
     you can teach them.

202. If there is one thing that has helped me as a
     coach, it's my ability to recognize winners, or
     good people who can become winners by
     paying a price.

MISTAKES

203. When you make a mistake, there are only
     three things you should ever do about it:
     admit it; learn from it; and don't repeat it.

204. I've made so many mistakes that if I don't make the same mistakes over, we're going to come pretty close to winning.

205. If a person doesn't help himself—if he isn't accountable for his own mistakes or oversights—he shouldn't expect others to help him either.

206. When I correct them in a meeting it's always "we" or "our" mistake, so they know it's a team deal, that we're responsible as a team. If I have to criticize, I like to start with something positive. Then when I've got their attention—they're always going to agree with you when you're telling 'em something good—I come back and say, "But boys, we are covering kickoffs like we're trying to live forever."

207. Win or lose, if you don't recognize the mistakes—mistakes in preparation, mistakes during a game—you're hurting yourself. I've been outcoached, too, and I sure don't forget those times. Do they live as long as the big victories? No. They live longer.

208. I'd do things differently now. I failed some of them [players], but it was all I knew at the time.

209. Don't worry about making mistakes—you're going to make mistakes. But don't make 'em mentally—make 'em wide open, and frequently that will be enough to carry you on through.

MOTIVATION

210. Motivating people—the ingredient that separates winners from losers.

211. You have to learn what makes this or that Sammy run. For one it's a pat on the back, for another it's eating him out, for still another it's a fatherly talk, or something else. You're a fool if you think as I did as a young coach, that you can treat them all alike.

212. I heard a coach say one time he'd rather have a whore kick his player out of bed and say, "Go get me some touchdowns," than for some little old sweet gal to say, "Be careful, now, and don't get hurt." That's a little salty, I suppose, but the message is plain.

213. Certainly [football] is still challenging—not the game itself, but the preparation, the planning, the practice, and, of course, the recruiting. However, the real challenge is creating a winning attitude in the players. The kind of feeling you can create on the practice field, the atmosphere around the dorm—these are the things that determine what kind of game you'll have.

214. We've been able to do more with ordinary players because we don't tell them they are ordinary. Our best teams usually had four or five great players and a lot of average ones.

215. You take those little rascals, talk to them good, pat them on the back, let them think they are good, and they will go out and beat the biguns.

216. If you whoop and holler all the time, the players just get used to it.

217. I know what it takes to win. If I can sell them on what it takes to win, then we are not going to lose too many football games.

OPTIMISM

218. There is always tomorrow, and tomorrow is the first day of the rest of our lives.

PEERS

219. I don't hire anybody not brighter than I am. If they're not brighter than I am, I don't need them.

PLANNING

220. Have a plan, not only for the day, but for the week and the month and the year and ten years from now. Anticipate. Plan. Anticipate every situation that could arise. Plan for every situation that could arise. Don't think second by second on what needs to be done. Have a plan. Follow the plan, and you'll be surprised how successful you can be. Most people don't plan. That's why it is easy to beat most folks.

221. I always had a plan I believed in so strongly that I thought it would win at Vassar College. I never doubted winning. It was just a question of how long it would take.

222. On the field I try not to make any decisions unless they have particular significance—I don't mean I sit there on my fat fanny, like I have done in some games, thinking or praying they would do it when I knew I should have—but I try to have a plan and the guts to stick to it no matter what happens.

223. I tell all my coaches you have to have a plan for everything, an objective; you just don't go out day to day and coach. You have a plan you believe in and you have to be strong enough not to compromise.

224. If you want to coach you have three rules to follow to win. One, surround yourself with people who can't live without football. I've had a lot of them. Two, be able to recognize winners. They come in all forms. And, three, have a plan for everything. A plan for practice, a plan for the game. A plan for being ahead, and a plan for being behind 20-0 at the half, with your quarterback hurt and the phones dead, with it raining cats and dogs and no rain gear because the equipment man left it at home.

POSTERITY

225. When people ask me what do I want to be remembered for, I have one answer: I want the people to remember me as a winner, 'cause I ain't never been nothing but a winner.

POTENTIAL

226. You try to make your team do something they're not capable of and you get murdered.

PRACTICE

227. Don't over-coach them. Let them play some. If you're out there coaching them all the time, when are they going to practice?

PRAISE

228. Bingo! That's a goodie!

(Comment he often used on his television show after a big hit)

229. He is the best punt catcher in America. I told him that when I gave him a hug when he came off the field. . . . I didn't know whether to hug him or choke him.

(Commenting on Joey Jones after his second fumbled punt in victory No. 315)

PREPARATION

230. You don't win those things [championships] in that last game against Auburn, and you don't win 'em in a bowl. They are won in August and early September, maybe even before that, in the summer, when the players are still at home.

231. Don't give up at halftime. Concentrate on winning the second half.

232. Don't look back, don't lose your guts, and teach your team to go out on the field and make things happen.

233. In terms of hours on the job, at Kentucky and Texas A&M and those first few years at Alabama, I would say it took every hour other than about the three in a twenty-four-hour day. The other three I just wasted—taking a little nap.

234. My approach to the game has been the same at all the places I've been. Vanilla. The sure way. That means, first of all, to win physically. If you got eleven on a field, and they beat the other eleven physically, they'll win. They will start forcing mistakes. They'll win in the fourth quarter.

235.
Expect the
unexpected.

An era nears an end as Coach Bryant beseeches his team in yet another clash against arch-rival Auburn. (AP/Wide World Photos)

236. You have to be willing to out-condition your opponents.

237. Formations don't win football games, people do. But they can give you an edge, and that's what coaches look for. That's why we change so much.

238. I was going to get in the first lick. That's the most important one. There might not be a second.

     (Speaking about a fight he got into in high school)

239. Don't get fancy. Every time you think, you weaken the team. Hit 'em! Show me some barnyard football.

240. Little things make the difference. Everyone is well prepared in the big things, but only the winners perfect the little things.

241. It's not the will to win that matters— everyone has that. It's the will to prepare to win that matters.

242. Scout yourself. Have a buddy who coaches scout you.

243. Common sense tells you the other guy will get careless, get sluggish mentally, and you'll beat him in the fourth quarter because you'll be alert for sudden changes, for blocked kicks and fumbles.

244. If a man is a quitter, I'd rather find out in practice than in a game. I ask for all a player has so I'll know later what I can expect.

245. We probably don't have as much fun during the week as some teams but we have more pleasant Saturdays than most.

246. Techniques alone don't win.

PRIDE

247. I don't know what it is, but I think it is catching!

248. I want a player with pride and one that knows what it takes to excel.

249. Always keep your heads up and act like champions.

QUITTING

250. Never quit. It is the easiest cop-out in the world. Set a goal and don't quit until you attain it. When you do attain it, set another goal, and don't quit until you reach it. Never quit.

251. I'll never give up on a player regardless of his ability as long as he never gives up on himself. In time he will develop.

252. The thing I try to encourage in our players is to never give up on themselves. I've had some that I've given up on, but they didn't give up on themselves, and they came through.

253. When the going gets tough, the tough get going.

254. The first time you quit, it's hard. The second time, it gets easier. The third time, you don't even have to think about it.

255. But there's one thing about quitters you have to guard against—they are contagious. If one boy goes, the chances are he'll take somebody with him, and you don't want that. So when they would start acting that way, I used to pack them up and get them out, or embarrass them, or do something to turn them around.

RECRUITING

256. The thing about recruiting is that you have to learn—and learn fast—that you can't make the chicken salad without the chicken.

257. Damn, the pickin's are slim.
    (Bryant's comment on signing a one-armed player, Murray Trimble at Texas A&M)

258. The best thing you have going for you in recruiting is a boy's mother.

259. A black newspaperman came up and started talking smart, like he was looking for something. He said, "How many black players you got on your team, Coach?" I said, "I don't have any. I don't have any white ones, I don't have any black ones. I just have football players. They come in all colors."

260. I tell my players they're special. They're something everybody should be proud of. They're not like the other students. I say, "If you were we'd have fifteen thousand out for football." You've got to take pride in being something special.

RESPECT

261. Don't worry about winning personality contests with your staff. You'd better worry about being respected. Anybody can be liked, a heck of a lot fewer respected.

262. I think a boy respects you more when you show him you're willing to sacrifice as much as you want him to.

RETIREMENT

263. Like my wife says, what the hell would I do to keep from going nuts?

264. If I miss coaching that much, I believe I could go to (this is the kind of job I've always wanted anyway for fun) I believe I could go to some little school and get a job, where they didn't recruit, where all the kids had wanted to come there since they were little children.

265. I'm the one who'll decide when my career is over. They won't have to ask me to quit the way they did Adolph Rupp. I'll know the time. As long as I'm getting those chills up my back, as long as I know I'm contributing toward another national championship, I'll be around. And the only way you can measure that is by winning. There's no other way.

ROLE MODELS

266. Remember you are representing a lot of people—your family, your school, your friends.

RULES

267. I believe if you have rules, you abide by them.

SACRIFICE

268. I don't think anyone can go to school, do well academically and athletically and do all the things other people do. You have to pass up a few things, not because I say so but because you have enough pride.

269. Everybody—and I mean coaches, players, managers, everybody—has to suck 'em up and work and scratch and pray and fight to win.

270. In any big game there are five or six or seven key plays that will decide the outcome. If you put out for five seconds on every play, you'll get your share of those key plays. You never know when they'll come, so you have to go all out every time.

271. If my 75-percent boy plays 15 percent over his ability and your 100-percent boy slogs around and plays 15 percent under his, then we will beat you every time.

SUCCESS

272. Remember, do your job for just six seconds, every play, and make something happen. Don't wait for it to happen. Make it happen. Do that, and we're going to win.

    (Pep talk before LSU game, 1964)

273. If you get ahead, then play like you're behind.

274. Intangibles. I can't even spell *intangible*, but I know you have to have it. When one man opens a business and goes broke and another man comes behind him and is a success with exactly the same business, that's intangibles.

275. Surround yourself with people that care, people that football means something to— assistant coaches, secretaries, ticket takers.

276. I want every one of you gentlemen to come by me on your way out, and shake hands and look in that mirror, because when you come back in here tonight you're going to look in it again. You'll have to decide then if you gave your best. And every morning you shave from now on you're going to think about giving your best, because I'm going to make you. I'm going to be reminding you.

(Pep talk to a Texas A&M team)

277. We're on a longer road. We've got a bigger [game] next week, and the week after. Because the next game is always more important if you're going to the top. And that's where we're going.

278. There's a lot of blood, sweat, and guts between dreams and success.

279. You're never beaten until the clock runs out.

TALENT

280. If you don't have the talent to win with talent alone, you have to compensate.

281. Find the talent and relate to it.

TEACHING

282. When folks are ignorant, you don't condemn them, you teach 'em.

283. Sacrifice. Work. Self-discipline. I teach these things, and my boys don't forget them when they leave.

284. No coach has ever won a game by what he knows; it's what his players know that counts.

285. The main thing is getting the material and teaching your kids to forget a losing complex. Teach them to win.

286. Kids are different, and you want different personalities around them. They can't all relate to one type. On the coaching end, there are blackboard coaches and there are field coaches, and a rare few who are both. With some it's not how much they know but how much they can teach.

287. We want our people to be something special.

TEAMWORK

288. One man doesn't make a team. It takes eleven.

289. People who are in it for their own good are individualists. They don't share the same heartbeat that makes a team so great. A great unit, whether it be football or any organization, shares the same heartbeat.

290. I told them my system was based on the "ant plan," that I'd gotten the idea watching a colony of ants in Africa during the war. A whole bunch of ants working toward a common goal.

(Commenting on his system that shook up the Southwest Conference during his years at Texas A&M)

One genuinely grizzled Bear. (AP/Wide World Photos)

291. If anything goes bad, I did it. If anything goes semi-good, we did it. If anything goes really good, then you did it. That's all it takes to get people to win football games for you.

292. I've told you a jillion times—the defenses or the coaches don't have anything to do with it, really. It's the people that play!

293. The player's abilities dictate what we do. I've had more great quarterbacks than all the other coaches put together, and half of that was pure luck.

294. We can't have two standards, one set for the dedicated young men who want to do something ambitious and one set for those who don't.

295. I'm just a plowhand from Arkansas, but I have learned over the years how to hold a team together—how to lift some men up, how to calm down others, until finally they've got one heartbeat, together, a team.

296. Teamwork—oneness as I like to call it. I don't think there has ever been a self-made man. I think it takes a team.

297. Team victory is more important than individual victory.

298. Get the winners into the game.

TIMING

299. Coach [Frank] Thomas knew what to say and when to say it, and that's the secret. Timing is everything.

300. Success in anything is a matter of timing, no matter what you do.

301. You go into your boss's office to ask for a raise, the timing better be right. You walk into the kitchen and give your wife a smack [kiss]. Sometimes it's just the thing to do, and she eats it up. Other times it don't mean a thing. You might as well kiss the refrigerator.

WINNING

302. Winning isn't everything, but it sure beats anything that comes in second.

303. There's no easy way to win, and the tougher it is the more they have to believe in you, and to trust you. Communication. It's the key to everything. You have to have it to win, and when you lose, too, so you can hold them in your hand.

304. When we're not in the running for number one, people know I haven't done my job.

305. I honestly believe that if you are willing to out-condition the opponent, have confidence in your ability, be more aggressive than your opponent and have a genuine desire for team victory, you will become the national champions. If you have all the above, you will acquire confidence and poise, and you will have those intangibles that win the close ones.

306. It is not an "I" thing, it is a "WE" thing.
(On win No. 315)

307. When you get eleven people trying to win on every play, you'll win.

308. A great performer can give a great performance and lose. A great player will do the things it takes to win.

309. Play 'em jaw to jaw, and you'll win in the fourth quarter.

310. When you're number one, you don't play for the tie.

311. If you don't at least try to win, you don't deserve the championship.

312. You've got to keep from losing before you can win. There is a difference between losing and getting beat. There is a difference between winning and beating people. If we keep from losing, the worst we'll come out with is a tie.

313. Winners [know how to relate to people]. I don't know whether it's knowledge or not. It's just something God gave some but didn't give to others. Some people are able to get along with people and organize this, that, and the other. Some are able to fly, swim, dive. Heck, I can't even swim.

314. I don't know if I'm smart enough to know how to describe a winner, but I guess I've been wise enough or maybe just lucky enough of being able to spot one. I know a winner has dedication and pride and the will to win, and he'll do a little bit extra every day to improve himself and his team. A winner is worried about his team and his school, and he'll outwork people, and he'll sacrifice.

315. I've always tried to stress to my players that they need to grow each day of their life in three important ways: mentally, physically, and spiritually. If they'd do that, they'll be all right.

316. If wanting to win is a fault, as some of my critics seem to insist, then I plead guilty. I like to win. I know no other way. It's in my blood.

317. Frankly, I'd just as soon play lousy if we could luck out and win that way.

318. I'm not sure we beat them, but we won. That's good enough.

319. What better way is there to build character, to instill pride, than to win?

320. When you go out and play a super-duper game, there is no way to pinpoint the reason.

321. Point out to them that they don't have to win, but there is a great difference in the reward from winning than in losing. A game that cannot be played over has to be lived with for life. Only special people win consistently. There is very little difference in being average and being a champion.

322. I've never had any complaints on winning.

323. If you believe in yourself and have dedication and pride—and never quit—you'll be a winner. The price of victory is high but so are the rewards.

BIBLIOGRAPHY

Bryant, Bear, *Young Athlete*. October 1980.

Bryant, Paul W., "Thirty Thoughts on an Airplane About Coaching the Game of Football." Speech at National High School Athletic Coaches' Association Convention. Colorado Springs, Co., 1972.

Bryant, Paul W., "Be Proud: Crimson Tide's Dr. Bryant Gives His Recipe for Living at MA Banquet"; Phillip Marshall, *Montgomery Advertiser*.

Bryant, Paul, and John Underwood, *Bear: The Hard Life and Good Times of Alabama's Coach Bryant.* Boston and Toronto: Little, Brown, and Co. (Sports Illustrated Books), 1972.

Bryant, Paul W., and John Underwood, *Bear: The Hard Life and Good Times of Alabama's Coach Bryant.* New York: Little, Brown, 1974.

Bynum, Mike, *Bryant: The Man, the Myth.* Atlanta: Cross Roads Books, 1979.

Cromartie, Bill, *Braggin' Rights*. Atlanta: Gridiron Publishers, 1978.

Dent, Jim, *The Junction Boys: How Ten Days in Hell with Bear Bryant Forged a Champion*. New York: St. Martin's, 1999.

Dunnavant, Keith, *Coach*. New York: Simon and Schuster, 1996.

Elebash, Camille, "Bear Bryant." *Sky*, October 1977.

Ford, Tommy, *Bama Under Bear: Alabama's Family Tides*. Huntsville, Ala.: Strode Publishers, 1983.

Frady, Marshall, "The Bear in Winter," *Sport*. September 1975.

Freeman, Criswell, *The Wisdom of Southern Football: Common Sense and Uncommon Genius from 101 Gridiron Greats*. Nashville, Tenn.: Walnut Grove Press, 1995.

Herskowitz, Mickey, *The Legend of Bear Bryant*. New York: McGraw-Hill, 1987.

Langford, George, *The Crimson Tide, Alabama Football*. Chicago: Harry Regency Co., 1974.

Lee, S. C., *Young Bear: The Legend of Bear Bryant's Boyhood*. Huntsville, Ala.: Strode Publishers, 1978.

Maikovich, Andrew J., *Sports Quotations: Maxims, Quips and Pronouncements for Writers and Fans*. Jefferson, N.C., and London: McFarland & Co., 1984.

Maisel, Ivan, "The Bear." *Don Heinrich's College Football*, 1991.

Marshall, Benny, *Winning Isn't Everything, But it Beats Anything That Comes in Second*. Nashville: Parthenon Press, 1983.

McKenzie, Mike, "The Bear: A Paradoxical Legend." *Memphis Press-Scimitar*, December 17, 1976 (reprinted from *Tuscaloosa News*).

Peterson, James A., and Bill Cromartie, *Bear Bryant: Countdown to Glory*. New York: Leisure Press, 1983.

Reed, Delbert, *Paul "Bear" Bryant: What Made Him A Winner*. Tuscaloosa: Visions Press, 1995.

Reflections, compiled by Bill Lumpkin. January 25, 1993.

Remembering Bear: The Life of Coach Paul "Bear" Bryant, 1913–1983. Birmingham, Ala.: *Birmingham News*, 1983.

Schoor, Gene, *100 Years of Alabama Football*. Atlanta: Longstreet Press, 1991.

Smith, E. S., *Bear Bryant: Football's Winning Coach*. New York: Walker and Co., 1984.

Stallings, Gene, *Bear Bryant on Winning Football*. Englewood Cliffs, N.J.: Prentice Hall, 1983. (originally published as *Building a Championship Football Team*, 1960)

Stoddard, Tom, *Turnaround: The Untold Story of Bear Bryant's First Year as Head Coach at Alabama*. Montgomery, Ala.: Black Belt Press, 1996.

Sugar, Bert Randolph, *The Book of Sports Quotes. A Treasury of the Most Outrageous Wit and Wisdom From Ali to Zimmer*. New York: Quick Fox; Music Sales Corp., 1979.

Woodley, Richard, *The Bear*. New York: Pocket Books, 1984.

INDEX